English Series

Prepositions, Conjunctions and Interjections

by S. Harold Collins

Book cover design by Kathy Kifer

Copyright © 1992 Stanley H. Collins

Published by:
Garlic Press
605 Powers St.
Eugene, OR 97402

ISBN 0-931993-43-1
Order Number GP-043

www.garlicpress.com

Dear Parents and Teachers,

The Straight Forward English Series has been designed for parents, teachers, and students. The Series is composed of books designed to measure, teach, review, and master specific English skills. The focus of this book is prepositions, conjunctions, and interjections.

What makes this Series Different?

- These are the preposition, conjunction, and interjection skills included in major school textbooks that all students must learn.

  Textbook series have been compared. The Straight Forward English Series presents the skills crucial to mastery of prepositions, conjunctions, and interjections as reflected in major English textbooks.

- Preposition, conjunction, and interjection skills are concisely explained, practiced, and tested.

- Mastery can be measured by comparing the Beginning Assessment Test with the Final Assessment Test.

- More content. No distracting or unrelated pictures or words. The skills are straightforward.

How to use this book.

- Give the Beginning Assessment Test to gain a starting measure of a student's preposition, conjunction, and interjection skills.

- Progress through each topic. Work the exercises. Exercise work can be done in the book or on a separate sheet of paper. Set a standard to move from one topic to the next. If the standard is not met, go back and refocus on that topic.

- Give the Final Assessment Test to gain an ending measure of a student's preposition, conjunction, and interjection skills. Compare the skill levels before and after the Final Assessment Test.

Contents

Beginning Assessment Test

A. Recognizing Prepositions
Insert a preposition to complete each sentence.

1. I went _____ the store.
2. She set the box _____ the table.
3. This book is _____ cats.
4. Daddy drinks a cup of coffee _____ the morning.
5. Annie wrote a letter _____ me.

B. Prepositional Phrases
Underline each prepositional phrase.

1. Candace went into the house.
2. She lives in California.
3. Mother likes going to the art galleries.
4. Barbara arrived during lunch.
5. Jonathan rode his bike up the hill.
6. The boy from Ireland spoke to our class.
7. The story about the monkey was my favorite.
8. The history of Oregon is very interesting.
9. I saw Jane at the supermarket.
10. They rode like the wind.

C. Conjunctions
Underline each conjunction.

1. Bob and Dan are brothers.
2. I exercise two or three times a week.
3. He likes the red car, but I like the white one.
4. The mailman comes whether it is raining or not.
5. He wanted to come, but he didn't have time.

D. Interjections
Underline the interjections in each sentence.

1. Wow! Did you see that?
2. "Gee," she said, "I didn't know he was coming."
3. My oh my! What a mess!
4. Ouch!
5. Stop! That hurt.

Prepositions

Recognizing Prepositions

A preposition is a word placed before a noun or pronoun to indicate its relationship to some other word in the sentence.

A preposition is followed by a noun or pronoun. That noun or pronoun is the **object of the preposition**.

•Most often used prepositions.

at	from	on
by	in	to
for	of	with

The store closes **at** midnight.
The letter is **in** the mailbox.
The letter is **for** you.

•Other common prepositions.

about	before	down	out
above	behind	during	over
across	below	inside	through
after	beside	into	under
around	between	near	until

They walked **around** the lake.
The dancers arrived **before** lunch.
(You) Walk **across** the street and **into** the store.
He looked **under** the table **near** the porch.

Exercise 1. Write three prepositions that could complete each sentence.

1. They waited - the phone.
2. She threw a rock - the creek.
3. The address was - the door.
4. The book - the table is mine.
5. Put them - the basket.

6. The cat sat - the dog.
7. Alice lives - the lake.
8. We'll go - school.
9. They talked - the show.
10. We stood - the boat.
11. She found them - the dresser.
12. We ate - the playground.
13. The children ran - me.
14. The house is - the hill - large trees.
15. Put the keys - the basket - the window.
16. The car is - the store.
17. The man sat - the blue car - the tree.
18. Apples are - the box.
19. Talk - me.
20. What is - the refrigerator?

Exercise 2. Underline the prepositions. Be alert. Three sentences do not have prepositions. Six sentences have at least two prepositions.

1. She walked to the window.
2. The books are on the table.
3. The juice is in the cupboard near the canned fruit.
4. I will call you the minute I know the answer.
5. What would you like with your cereal?
6. They met by the pond in the park.
7. Ira arrived at exactly ten o'clock.
8. We live behind a grove of trees.
9. The search and rescue patrol finished early.
10. Our family arrived after everyone had left.
11. They slept during the entire parade.
12. We couldn't leave without them.
13. Your coat is on the seat in our car.
14. Jean put the boxes under the table.
15. They walked through the gate and into the yard.
16. He left the very next day.
17. She returned after midnight.
18. They drove to the house in the country.
19. What is between those trees?
20. Put it in your backpack.

Prepositions

Object of the Preposition

The noun or pronoun that follows a preposition is the **object of the preposition**.

The preposition connects the object (the noun or pronoun) to another word in the sentence.

These sample sentences have the preposition and its object underlined. Remember, the object of the preposition is the first noun or pronoun after the preposition.

> Andrew gave it to me.
> The call is for Jane.
> They walked into the room.
> Elena parked beside the large green house.
> They rode to the park and walked across the bridge.

Exercise 1. The preposition is underlined. Circle the noun or pronoun that is the object of the preposition.

1. I was standing in line.
2. Put your bike against the wall.
3. You can't go beyond the next house.
4. Can you walk around it?
5. They brought the food into the large kitchen.
6. Elise sat between us.
7. She walked to the door and called to me.
8. Ari walked toward the door.
9. He phoned from New York City.
10. Our house is beyond the church.
11. Bring it into the bright light.
12. I am afraid of dogs.
13. My aunt arrived during lunch.
14. Your fingerprints are on the bedroom window.
15. Our house is among elm trees.

4

Exercise 2. Underline both the preposition and the object of the preposition.

1. Who lives across the street?
2. I have a good picture of my house.
3. Mother sat behind them.
4. Our house is beyond your house.
5. I put my book under the chair in your kitchen.
6. I rode home by myself.
7. The house near the store is red.
8. The book beneath the boxes is mine.
9. They arrived at six o'clock.
10. I came to school earlier today.
11. We have been here since yesterday.
12. They could not leave without it.
13. Edgar called from the neighbor's house.
14. He came for a special occasion.
15. Look in the box near the back door.

Exercise 3. Underline both the preposition and the object, if any.

1. June is in love with Jeff.
2. Have you driven to the Coast?
3. I think the waves on the Oregon Coast are outstanding.
4. I'm over here in the bushes.
5. How old will you be on your next birthday?
6. They're staying for the weekend.
7. Don and Jane are coming to our house on Friday.
8. Barbara, come here please.
9. I need your help with this math problem.
10. It's a really tough one.
11. I took some pictures with my new camera.
12. They came out very well.
13. Can we go for ice cream?
14. Yes, in a minute.
15. Do you have any in your refrigerator?

Prepositions

Prepositional Phrases

A **prepositional phrase** is a group of words that begins with a preposition and ends with an object.

Our dog sleeps <u>under the dining room table</u>.
The bicycle <u>in the garage</u> is <u>near the door</u>.

A preposition will always be part of a prepositional phrase. A prepositional phrase must have at least two words, the preposition and its object.

Here are four common patterns of prepositional phrases. Combinations of these patterns expand sentences and make expression greater.

1. Preposition + noun.

   He drove <u>to work</u>.
2. Preposition + pronoun.

   Alice gave it <u>to her</u>.
3. Preposition + article + noun.

   He drove <u>to the store</u>.
4. Preposition + article + modifier + noun.(Modifiers are adjectives and
   He drove <u>across the frozen lake</u>.   adverbs)

Exercise 1. Underline the entire prepositional phrase. Some sentences will have more than one prepositional phrase.

1. We talked on the phone.
2. They drive to work.
3. The children hid under the bench near you.
4. We crept down the stairs.
5. Emily will give it to me.
6. They asked many questions about it.
7. We rented a cabin at Lost Lake.
8. We traveled through a long tunnel.
9. The top of the ridge was covered with fir and pine trees.
10. The mountains sloped toward the ocean.
11. They rose before dawn and came with us.
12. We hiked for six miles.

6

13. The package on the desk by the door is mine.
14. The speaker talked for two long hours.
15. The small cat scampered across the porch.

Exercise 2. Underline the entire prepositional phrase. Underline the object a second time. Several sentences have more than one prepositional phrase.

1. The deer ate from her hand.
2. The ivy grew along the fence.
3. They couldn't wait until the last moment.
4. The letter is on the window sill.
5. The car is inside the garage.
6. I will write to them.
7. We will arrive in two hours by air.
8. They had been looking for her.
9. Call me in the morning before lunch.
10. I will cook dinner for myself in a few minutes.
11. We remained in the house after the storm.
12. They walked through the doors and between two beds.
13. My brother crawled over the entire hedge.
14. I went across it and over the end.
15. Is there a prepositional phrase in this sentence?

Exercise 3. Complete the chart for these sentences. Sentence 1 is done as an example.

1. My brother arrived with his new friend.

	Prepositional Phrase	Preposition	Object	Pattern
1.	With a friend	with	friend	preposition + article + noun #3

2. The letter was given to him on Thursday.
3. You will hand it to them.
4. You must leave before midnight.
5. Jane walked through the door into the yard.
6. I had an extra with me in a large bag.
7. The sheep were under a shade tree.
8. The dog ran to me without a sound.
9. It is on the living room table.
10. Let's look around the room.

Prepositions

Prepositional Phrases as Adjectives

An entire prepositional phrase can act as an adjective if it modifies a noun or pronoun.

A prepositional phrase can act as an adjective. You already know that adjectives are words that describe nouns or pronouns. Prepositional phrases can also describe nouns or pronouns.

A <u>newspaper</u> story described his life.

A story <u>in the newspaper</u> described his life.

A prepositional phrase that acts like an adjective usually follows the noun or pronoun it modifies.

Here are other examples:

The girl <u>in the red coat</u> lives here. (Which girl?)
The story <u>about the monkey</u> was very funny. (What kind of story?)
Our friend <u>from Australia</u> stayed two weeks.
We enjoyed the museums <u>of art and natural history</u>.
The flower shop sold books <u>about different kinds of flowers.</u>

The last example shows you how prepositional phrases can be linked together to tell (describe as adjectives do) more. Good writers and speakers use prepositional phrases efficiently to tell as much as possible without being too wordy.

Exercise 1. Rewrite these sentences. Add a prepositional phrase that will modify the underlined noun or pronoun.

1. The <u>history</u> is interesting.
2. The <u>hat</u> belongs here.
3. She knows the <u>woman</u>.
4. I read a <u>story</u>.
5. A <u>map</u> was helpful.
6. Elena called her <u>sister</u>.
7. He of all <u>people</u> knew the answer. (Add a second prepositional phrase)
8. The <u>train</u> left the station.

9. The <u>glass</u> was broken.
10. Your <u>book</u> is the best book.
11. He has <u>one</u>.
12. The travelers need a <u>bag</u>.
13. My <u>cat</u> sits on the back fence.
14. The <u>book</u> was closed.
15. Who has been reading a <u>book</u>?

Exercise 2. Underline the prepositional phrases that modify nouns or pronouns. Draw an arrow to the noun or pronoun that the prepositional phrase modifies.

1. I read a story about ancient China.
2. The answer to the question is obvious.
3. The key on the table near the door is mine.
4. Their level of understanding is not good.
5. The house on the hill with trees is vacant.
6. The store across the street is also vacant.
7. The cat on the sofa lives across the street. (Careful: Does "across the street" modify a noun?)
8. The man over there left the box of fruit.
9. The dishes on the table were dirty.
10. Did you see the display of wooden toys?
11. Our neighbor around the corner works downtown.
12. The flowers between the fence and sidewalk are weeds.
13. The map by your arm is the best map in town.
14. The letter from my parents arrived yesterday.
15. Children of all ages attend the show.

Exercise 3. Most of the sentences contain incorrect prepositions. Identify them and insert a better preposition of your own.

1. Come over at my house.
2. The car crashed onto the tree.
3. My brother loves hiking in the woods.
4. Set the dishes over the table.
5. I read a story in Chinese history.
6. There's a mosquito to your arm.
7. The old man put his hat above his head.
8. That girl has long hair up to her shoulders.
9. The movie playing about that theater is scary.
10. There's an airplane flying up your head.

Prepositions

Prepositional Phrases as Adverbs

An entire prepositional phrase can act as an adverb if it modifies a verb.

A prepositional phrase functioning as an adverb can tell "when," "where," or "how" something happens.

> They rode <u>on a bus</u>. (Rode how?)
>
> Our guests arrived <u>at night</u>. (Arrived when?)
>
> The story begins <u>in Canada</u>. (Begins where?)
>
> We walked <u>to church</u> <u>at a slow pace</u>. (Walked where? Walked how?)

Prepositional phrases that describe verbs usually follow the verbs they describe.

Exercise 1. Rewrite these sentences. Add a prepositional phrase that will modify the underlined verb.

1. They <u>rode</u>.
2. Our team <u>won</u>.
3. The cat from next door <u>hid</u>.
4. The clerk <u>returned</u>.
5. Baseball <u>is enjoyed</u>.
6. The bird <u>flew</u>.
7. Emily <u>called</u> a friend.
8. She <u>talked</u> about animals.
9. The car <u>is used</u>.
10. We <u>are studying</u> about India.

Sentences 8 and 10 could have been tricky. They already contained a prepositional phrase modifying a verb. You were to provide another prepositional phrase to modify the verbs in each sentence. Here could have been two answers:

> She talked <u>for two hours</u> about animals.
>
> We are studying <u>in school</u> about India.

If you supplied a prepositional phrase that modified *animals* or *India*, would the prepositional phrase you supplied have been adverbial? No. The prepositional phrase would have modified a noun and, thus, have been an adjective modifying a prepositional phrase. For instance:

> She talked about animals <u>of all sizes</u>.
> We are studying about India <u>during 1920</u>.

How you use a prepositional phrase is important to express exactly what you mean.

Example 2. Underline any prepositional phrases that modify a verb. Draw an arrow to the verb that the prepositional phrase modifies.

1. The class rode on a bus.
2. The ride was two hours long.
3. Buses by the dozen leave from the station.
4. Buses come in many colors.
5. We stopped at the store and bought lunch.
6. We learned everything from our field trip.
7. The mouse sat in a cage by itself.
8. It can run within an enormous wheel.
9. Sometimes it plays on the kitchen floor.
10. It sleeps during the day and plays at night.
11. My brother ran beyond the sign.
12. The bridge will be built across the river.
13. The smoke was seen from thirty miles.
14. We played after dinner in the park.
15. The nurse ran across the street.

Did you find that sentences 3, 7, 8, 10, and 14 each had several prepositional phrases? Sentence 3 used prepositional phrases as adjectives and adverbs.

> Buses <u>by the dozen</u> leave <u>from the station</u>.

Sentences 7, 8, 10 and 14 contained two prepositional phrases that were used as adverb phrases.

The mouse sat <u>in a cage</u> <u>by itself.</u>
It can run <u>within an enormous wheel</u> <u>for exercise.</u>
It sleeps <u>during the day</u> and plays <u>at night</u>.
We played <u>after dinner</u> <u>in the park</u>.

Exercise 3. Combine these sentences with prepositional phrases to make one sentence. Sentence 1 is done as an example.

1. Children from everywhere came.
   Children came at noon.
   Children from everywhere came at noon.

2. My friend lives next door.
   My friend lives in a grey house.
3. I can work by myself.
   I can work without any help.
4. John and I walked from our house to the store.
   John and I walked in the snow to the store.
5. The house on the hill was vacant.
   The house was vacant for several years.
6. Everyone in the crowd cheered.
   Everyone cheered at once.

Exercise 4. Underline all prepositional phrases. Tell whether each works as an adjective or an adverb.

1. The house down the street is vacant.
2. They painted the house with an awful color.
3. Shoes come in many sizes.
4. The game lasted until dark.
5. The biggest animal in the store was a St. Bernard.
6. It sat alone in a corner behind some boxes.
7. The history of China during the last six years is interesting.
8. We washed the car in a hurry.
9. The glass over the door is fragile.
10. His eyes filled with delight.

Prepositions

Faulty Reference

A prepositional phrase must clearly refer to the word it modifies.

We have learned two simple patterns for prepositional phrases:
- Subject + prepositional phrase + verb
    The house across the street is vacant.

- Subject + verb + prepositional phrase
    The house was vacant until last week.

Prepositional phrases usually follow the noun or pronoun they modify (adjective prepositional phrase) or prepositional phrases usually follow the verb they modify (adverb prepositional phrase).

When prepositional phrases that modify nouns or pronouns follow the wrong noun or pronoun, there is confusion:

- The boy went to the doctor with a broken arm.

Who has a broken arm? The boy or the doctor? The sentence should be:

    The boy with the broken arm went to the doctor.

- She gave cookies to my friends with nuts in them.

Do the friends have nuts? Or do the cookies? The sentence should be:

    She gave cookies with nuts in them to my friends.

Confusion also occurs when a prepositional phrase does not follow the verb it modifies.

To avoid any confusion, place prepositional phrases as close as possible to the noun, pronoun, or verb they modify.

Exercise 1. Rewrite each sentence. Place prepositional phrases correctly.

1. My mother at the age of two took me to Paris, France.
2. The cat ran from the bee with the long tail.
3. Ice cream was served to guests in paper cups.
4. Students visited their parents in high school.
5. I gave the book to my father about fishing.
6. The man ran into a tree on skis.
7. Put the hat on your head with a red feather.
8. She shouted at the cows that mooed with an accent.
9. The woman met the boy in the blue dress.
10. The thief was arrested by the officer in the stolen car.
11. The patient went to the dentist with cavities.
12. The answer was wrong to the question.
13. The dog was barking at the boy in the doghouse.
14. The house is next to the lake with the green door.
15. The car belongs to my friend without a seat.

Conjunctions

Coordinating Conjunctions

Conjunctions connect words or groups of words.
Coordinating conjunctions connect words or groups of words
that have equal rank.

Coordinating conjunctions connect, for example, nouns with nouns, verbs
with verbs, adjectives with adjectives, and adverbs with adverbs. Coordinating conjunctions cannot connect words of unequal rank, for example: nouns
with verbs, or adjectives with adverbs.

The most common coordinating conjunctions are **and**, **or**, **but**, **nor**.

•Coordinating Words of Equal Rank:

Nouns	**Elena** <u>and</u> **Emily** are sisters.
Verbs	You can **run** <u>or</u> **walk** to school.
Adjectives	The **beautiful** <u>but</u> **small** statue is expensive.
Adverbs	They walked **quickly** <u>and</u> **silently**.

•Coordinating Groups of Words of Equal Rank:

Prepositional phrases	We will move **in late spring** <u>or</u> **in early summer**.
Sentences	**My friend made a lunch**, <u>and</u> **I ate it**.
Adjectives + adverbs	She is **surprisingly small**, <u>but</u> **amazingly quick**.
Words in a series	You can **read**, **write**, <u>or</u> **rest** before you go.

Coordinating conjunctions help us to connect a variety of words and word
groups. When we can connect a variety of words or word groups, we can
express our thoughts quickly and with greater variation.

For instance, which of the following is easier to use?

Emily and Elena walked two miles to the store.
　　　or
Emily walked two miles to the store. Elena walked two miles to the store.

If you would care to speak or write one sentence rather than two, you will appreciate how coordinating conjunctions connect words.

Exercise 1. Use the coordinating conjunction that is supplied for each sentence to connect the appropriate nouns and verbs.

1. My neighbor has a dog.   (and)
   My neighbor has a cat.
2. I don't care if you come.   (or)
   I don't care if you go.
3. Cars move swiftly.   (and)
   Trucks move swiftly.
4. Our sick cat eats.   (and)
   Our sick cat sleeps.
5. The glasses were washed.
   The glasses were dried.   (and)
   The dishes were washed.
   The dishes were dried.

Exercise 2. Use coordinating conjunctions to connect these prepositional phrases.

1. The house was near the market.   (and)
   The house was near the playground.
2. Is it warmer in the north?   (or)
   Is it warmer in the south?
3. Our house is made from pine.   (and)
   Our house is made from fir.
4. Are you going by car?   (or)
   Are you going by airplane?
5. Jane arrived late.   (but)
   Elena arrived early.

Exercise 3. Circle the conjunction. Underline the words or groups of words that it connects.

1. I am going to the movie, but John is going swimming.
2. You must look under the bed and in the drawers.
3. She cut and split the wood.
4. Ellen or George finished the project.
5. The kitten was bright and alert.
6. He put the dishes on the table, and I put the bowls in the cupboard.
7. The large and friendly dog loved children.
8. She called and made an appointment.
9. The hat is on the table or near the door.
10. We left, and they came.

16

Conjunctions
Correlative Conjunctions

Correlative conjunctions are like other conjunctions except they are used in pairs. And like other conjunctions they connect words or groups of words.

Common correlative conjunctions are:

either...or	neither...nor
both...and	whether...or (not)

Exercise 1. Underline the correlative conjunctions in these sentences.

1. Either you go or I go.
2. Both buses and trains arrive at this station.
3. Neither dawn nor dusk is a convenient time to leave.
4. She both speaks and writes well.
5. He was neither tall nor frail.
6. You can have either three or four pieces.
7. Neither teacher nor student was prepared.
8. My answer depends upon whether you come or go.
9. His work is both neat and accurate.
10. Homes both in the valley and on the hillside were damaged.

Conjunctions

Subordinate Conjunctions

Subordinate conjunctions join clauses of unequal value. Subordinate conjunctions join dependent clauses to independent clauses.

Subordinating conjunctions connect groups of words (clauses) that have both a subject and predicate.

> I arrived when you left.
>
> When it was time to go, we packed.

•Common subordinating conjunctions are:

after	if
although	since
as, as if	when, whenever
because	where, wherever
before	while
	until

Subordinating conjunctions can be at the beginning of a sentence, in which case a comma will follow closely, or in the middle of a sentence.

> **Because** today is Wednesday, I will be late.
> or
> I will be late **because** today is Wednesday.

Exercise 1. Underline the subordinating conjunction.

1. Whenever you call, I'll be at home.
2. We can call after the mail arrives.
3. He simply likes to go because the movies are entertaining.
4. As you know, she is the best doctor.
5. Leave the garbage where it belongs.
6. The baby must crawl before he walks.

7. Abraham has worked here since he graduated,
8. If you behave yourself, you may come.
9. I can't come until I finish my homework.
10. While you were asleep, your brother went shopping.

Exercise 2. Conjunctions Review. Underline <u>all</u> conjunctions.

1. She was able to bring knives and forks but not cups and saucers.
2. After you called, the package arrived.
3. Do this while you are waiting.
4. Neither the mayor nor the council understood the problem.
5. I'm coming along because I like the walk.
6. They have known me since I was a baby.
7. Put the pillows on the bed and the blankets in the closet.
8. We'll do it tomorrow before they arrive.
9. Elena or Emily will make and deliver the gifts.
10. The comparison is either right or wrong.

Interjections

An **interjection** is a word or group of words that expresses a strong feeling. Interjections do not depend on other words in a sentence.

Interjections are followed either by an exclamation (!) point or a comma (,).

Strongest feelings are always followed by an exclamation mark.

> Oh, no! You can't do that.
> Hey! Did you see that?
> Ouch! That hurt!
> My goodness! I was surprised.

Notice that these short expressions of strong feeling stand alone. Anything else is separate and begins with a capital letter.

Milder feelings are followed by a comma.

> No, you must finish your work first.
> My goodness, this is difficult work.
> Wow, aren't you glad we've finished?

Remember, use an exclamation point for strong feelings or emotions and a comma for a lesser feeling or emotion.

And also remember, interjections are only one or two words.

Here are other common interjections.

Aha!	Whew!	Good grief!
Great!	Yes!	Ouch!
Oh!	Hurray!	Help!

Exercise 1. Underline all interjections in each sentence.

1. That was a close call. Whew!
2. Good! This is the right part.
3. Ah, ha! I caught that pesky mouse.
4. Wow, I can't believe I'm going. Fantastic!
5. He yelled, "Stop!"
6. Goodness, without you it would have been impossible.
7. Hey! Watch where you put that.
8. Alas, John didn't believe me.
9. She replied, "Yes, I am amazed too."
10. Help! Get me out of here!

Exercise 2. Choose an interjection for each sentence. Use each word once.

Oh	Hello	Gee	Oops	Oh, no
Quiet	Good-bye	Bravo	My oh my!	Unbelievable

1. _____ ! What a beautiful morning.
2. _____ , I haven't seen you for so long.
3. _____ , tell me more.
4. _____ ! I made a mistake.
5. _____ ! You can't do that.
6. Did you see that? _____ !
7. _____ , I thought I heard something.
8. _____ , see you next week.
9. The crowd shouted, "_____ !"
10. _____ ! What a surprise!

Exercise 3. Supply an interjection for each sentence. Use the correct punctuation.

1. _____ I skinned my elbow.
2. _____ What a fine job!
3. _____ That animal is dangerous.
4. _____ We're next?
5. _____ What a tall building.
6. _____ , that's no way to treat your cat.
7. _____ Is that true?
8. _____ , it's getting late.
9. _____ , algebra can be confusing.
10. _____ This box is heavy.

Final Assessment Test

Recognizing Prepositions

A. Find the prepositions. Underline them.

    1.   He got home about noon.
    2.   We returned home too late for lunch.
    3.   She stood behind the counter with her hands clasped.
    4.   My mother was beside herself with worry.
    5.   Take this package to the post office, please.

B. The prepositional phrases in the following sentences are underlined. Draw an
   arrow to the word each phrase modifies.

    1.   I read <u>about the game</u>.
    2.   It was <u>in the newspaper</u> <u>in the Sports Section</u>.
    3.   There was a picture <u>of Coach Fletcher</u> <u>from the high school</u>.
    4.   Everybody <u>in town</u> was proud <u>of the team</u>.
    5.   I'm trying out <u>for the team</u> <u>in the Spring</u>.

C. Correct and rewrite the following faulty references.

    1.   The puppy ran after the children with floppy ears.
    2.   The little girl went swimming in the pond with a pony tail.
    3.   A friend gave a speech to the assembly from my English class.
    4.   My brother laughed in the last row at my sister.
    5.   Dana will be in about five years old enough to drive.

Recognizing Conjunctions

A. Identify the coordinating conjunctions. Underline them.

    1.   My neighbor has two cats and a dog.
    2.   I like playing baseball and reading books.
    3.   My mother went to the store, but Daddy went to the gas station.
    4.   Are you from Canada or the United States?
    5.   She said I could go to the movies, the play, or the symphony.

B. Identify the correlative conjunctions. Underline them.

1. Either my sister comes with us, or I stay home.
2. He was neither short nor tall, neither fat nor thin.
3. We weren't sure whether or not he agreed with us.
4. Annie and Bart both sat down.
5. You can get either A or B on your report card, but no C.

C. Identify the subordinating conjunctions. Underline them.

1. My mother went to the store while Daddy went to the gas station.
2. I can drive a car when I'm sixteen.
3. Wherever I go, I meet the nicest people.
4. You may go to the movies if you finish your homework.
5. Donna couldn't go because she didn't finish her homework.

Recognizing Interjections

A. Use your own interjections to finish these sentences.

1. _____ ! We won the pennant.
2. _____! Bob asked Patricia to the Prom.
3. _____ . I broke the window with my baseball.
4. Look at the butterfly. _____ !
5. _____! That cake sure looks good.

ANSWERS

Beginning Assessment Test, Page 1.

A. Recognizing Prepositions
Insert a preposition to complete each sentence.

Answers may vary, but the following may be used as a guide:

1. into
2. on
3. about

4. in
5. to

1. I went _____ the store.
2. She set the box _____ the table.
3. This book is _____ cats.
4. Daddy drinks a cup of coffee _____ the morning.
5. Annie wrote a letter _____ me.

B. Prepositional Phrases
Underline each prepositional phrase.

1. Candace went into the house.
2. She lives in California.
3. Mother likes going to the art galleries.
4. Barbara arrived during lunch.
5. Jonathan rode his bike up the hill.
6. The boy from Ireland spoke to our class.
7. The story about the monkey was my favorite.
8. The history of Oregon is very interesting.
9. I saw Jane at the supermarket.
10. They rode like the wind.

C. Conjunctions
Underline each conjunction.

1. Bob and Dan are brothers.
2. I exercise two or three times a week.
3. He likes the red car, but I like the white one.
4. The mailman comes whether it is raining or not.
5. He wanted to come, but he didn't have time.

D. Interjections
Underline the interjections in each sentence.

1. <u>Wow</u>! Did you see that?
2. "<u>Gee</u>," she said, "I didn't know he was coming."
3. <u>My oh my</u>! What a mess!
4. <u>Ouch</u>!
5. <u>Stop</u>! That hurt.

• Prepositions, Exercise 1. Page 2.
    Answers may vary, but the following may be used as a guide:

1. by	6. beside	11. on	16. at
2. into	7. near	12. at	17. in, under
3. on	8. to	13. to	18. in
4. on	9. during	14. on, near	19. to
5. in	10. beside	15. in, by	20. in

• Prepositions, Exercise 2. Page 3.

1. to	6. by, in	11. during	16. *(none)*
2. on	7. at	12. without	17. after
3. in, near	8. behind, of	13. on, in	18. to, in
4. *(none)*	9. *(none)*	14. under	19. between
5. with	10. after	15. through, into	20. in

• Object of the Preposition, Exercise 1. Page 4.

1. line	6. us	11. light
2. wall	7. door, me	12. dogs
3. house	8. door	13. lunch
4. it	9. New York City	14. window
5. kitchen	10. church	15. trees

• Object of the Preposition, Exercise 2 . Page 5.

1. across, street	6. by, myself	11. since, yesterday
2. of, house	7. near, store	12. without, it
3. behind, them	8. beneath, boxes	13. from, house
4. beyond, house	9. at, six o'clock	14. for, occasion
5. under, chair/in, kitchen	10. to, school	15. in, box/near, door

• Object of a Preposition, Exercise 3 . Page 5.

1. in > love/with > Jeff
2. to > Coast
3. on > Oregon Coast
4. over > here/in > bushes
5. on > birthday
6. for > weekend
7. to > house/on>Friday
8. *(none)*
9. with > problem
10. *(none)*
11. with > Camera
12. *(none)*
13. from, house
14. for > ice cream
15. in > refrigerator

• Prepositional Phrases, Exercise 1. Page 6.

1. on the phone
2. to work
3. under the bench, near you
4. down the stairs
5. to me
6. about it
7. at Lost Lake
8. through a long tunnel
9. of the ridge, with fir and pine trees
10. toward the ocean
11. before dawn, with us
12. for > miles
13. on the desk, by the door
14. for two long hours
15. across the porch

• Prepositional Phrases, Exercise 2. Page 7.

1. from her <u>hand</u>
2. along the <u>fence</u>
3. until the last <u>moment</u>
4. on the window <u>sill</u>
5. inside the <u>garage</u>
6. to <u>them</u>
7. in two <u>hours</u>, by <u>air</u>
8. for <u>her</u>
9. in the <u>morning</u>, before <u>lunch</u>
10. for <u>myself</u>, in a few <u>minutes</u>
11. in the <u>house</u>, after the <u>storm</u>
12. through the <u>doors</u>, between two <u>beds</u>
13. over the entire <u>hedge</u>
14. across <u>it</u>, over the <u>end</u>
15. in this <u>sentence</u>

• Prepositional Phrases, Exercise 3. Page 7.

	Prep. Phrase	Prep.	Object	Pattern
2.	to him	to	him	prep + pronoun
	on Thursday	on	Thursday	prep + noun
3.	to them	to	them	prep + pronoun
4.	before midnight	before	midnight	prep + noun
5.	through the door	through	door	prep + article + noun
	into the yard	into	yard	prep + article + noun
6.	with me	with	me	prep + pronoun
	in a large bag	in	bag	prep + article + modifier + noun

Prep. Phrase	Prep.	Object	Pattern
7. under a shade tree	under	tree	prep + article + modifier + noun
8. to me	to	me	prep + pronoun
without a sound	without	sound	prep + article + noun
9. on the living room table	on	table	prep + article + modifiers + noun
10. around the room	around	room	prep + article + noun

• Prepositional Phrases as Adjectives, Exercise 1. Page 8.

Answers will vary, but we'll give you examples for the first three:

1.   The history <u>of American Asians</u> is interesting.
2.   The hat <u>with the red feather</u> belongs here.
3.   She knows the woman <u>in the black limousine</u>.

• Prepositional Phrases as Adjectives, Exercise 2. Page 9.

1. about Ancient China > *story*
2. to the question > *answer*
3. on the table > *key*
   near the door > *table*
4. of understanding > *level*
5. on the hill > *house*
   with trees > *hill*
6. across the street > *store*
7. on the sofa > *cat*
8. over there > *man*
   of fruit > *box*
9. on the table > *dishes*
10. of wooden toys > *display*
11. around the corner > *neighbor*
12. between the fence >*flowers*
13. by your arm > *map*, in town> *map*
14. from my parents > *letter*
15. of all ages > *children*

• Prepositional Phrases as Adjectives, Exercise 3. Page 9.

1. to my house
2. into the tree
3. in the woods
4. on the table
5. about Chinese history
6. on your arm
7. on his head
8. down to her shoulders
9. at that theater
10. over your head

• Prepositional Phrases as Adverbs, Exercise 1. Page 10.

   Answers will vary, but we'll give you examples for the first three.

   1.   They <u>rode</u> *on the subway.*
   2.   Our team <u>won</u> *by three points.*
   3.   The cat from next door <u>hid</u> *under the house.*

• Prepositional Phrases as Adverbs, Exercise 2. Page 11.

   1. on a bus > *rode*
   2. *(none)*

   3. from the station > *leave*
   4. in many colors > *come*
   5. at the store > *stopped*
   6. from our field trip > *learned*

   7. in a cage > *sat*/ by itself > *sat*
   8. within an enormous wheel > *can run*

   9. on the kitchen floor > *plays*
   10. during the day > *sleeps* /at night > *plays*
   11. beyond the sign > *ran*
   12. across the river > *will be built*
   13. from thirty miles > *was seen*
   14. after dinner > *played* / in the park> *played*
   15. across the street > *ran*

• Prepositional Phrases as Adverbs, Exercise 3. Page 12.

   1.   Children from everywhere came at noon.
   2.   My friend lives next door in a grey house.
   3.   I can work by myself without any help.
   4.   John and I walked in the snow from our house to the store.
   5.   The house on the hill was vacant for several years.
   6.   Everyone in the crowd cheered at once.

• Prepositional Phrases as Adverbs or Adjectives, Exercise 4. Page 12.

   1. The house <u>down the street</u> is vacant. **(Adj.)**
   2. They painted the house <u>with an awful color</u>. **(Adv.)**
   3. Shoes come <u>in many sizes</u>. **(Adv.)**
   4. The game lasted <u>until dark</u>. **(Adv.)**
   5. The biggest animal <u>in the store</u> was a St. Bernard. **(Adj.)**
   6. It sat alone <u>in a corner</u> <u>behind some boxes</u>. **(Adv. / Adv.)**
   7. The history <u>of China</u> <u>during the last six years</u> is interesting. **(Adj. / Adj.)**
   8. We washed the car <u>in a hurry</u>. **(Adv.)**
   9. The glass <u>over the door</u> is fragile. **(Adj.)**
   10. His eyes filled <u>with delight</u>. **(Adv.)**

• Faulty Reference, Exercise 1. Page 14.

1. My mother took me to Paris, France at the age of two.
2. The cat with the long tail ran from the bee.
3. Ice cream in paper cups was served to guests.
4. Students in high school visited their parents.
5. I gave the book about fishing to my father.
6. The man on skis ran into a tree.
7. Put the hat with a red feather on your head.
8. She shouted with an accent at the cows that mooed.
9. The woman in the blue dress met the boy.
10. The thief in the stolen car was arrested by the officer.
11. The patient with cavities went to the dentist.
12. The answer to the question was wrong.
13. The dog in the doghouse was barking at the boy.
14. The house with the green door is next to the lake.
15. The car without a seat belongs to my friend.

• Coordinating Conjunctions, Exercise 1. Page 16.

1. My neighbor has a dog and a cat.
2. I don't care if you come or go.
3. Cars and trucks move swiftly.
4. Our sick cat eats and sleeps.
5. The glasses and dishes were washed and dried.

• Coordinating Conjunctions, Exercise 2. Page 16.

1. The house was near the market and the playground.
2. Is it warmer in the north or in the south?
3. Our house is made from pine and fir.
4. Are you going by car or by airplane?
5. Jane arrived late, but Elena arrived early.

• Coordinating Conjunctions, Exercise 3. Page 16.

1. I am going to the movie, **but** John is going swimming.
2. You must look under the bed **and** in the drawers.
3. She cut **and** split the wood.
4. Ellen **or** George finished the project.
5. The kitten was bright **and** alert.
6. He put the dishes on the table, **and** I put the bowls in the cupboard.
7. The large **and** friendly dog loved children.
8. She called **and** made an appointment.
9. The hat is on the table **or** near the door.
10. We left, **and** they came.

• Correlative Conjunctions, Exercise 1. Page 17.

1. Either...or
2. Both...and
3. Neither...nor
4. both...and
5. neither...nor

6. either...or
7. Neither...nor
8. whether...or
9. both...and
10. both...and

• Subordinating Conjunctions, Exercise 1. Page 18.

1. Whenever
2. after
3. because
4. As
5. where

6. before
7. since
8. If
9. until
10. While

• Conjunctions Review, Exercise 1. Page 19.

1. and / but / and
2. After
3. while
4. Neither...nor
5. because

6. since
7. and
8. before
9. or / and
10. either...or

• Interjections, Exercise 1. Page 21.

1. Whew!
2. Good!
3. Ah, ha!
4. Wow, / Fantastic!
5. Stop!

6. Goodness,
7. Hey!
8. Alas,
9. Yes,
10. Help!

• Interjections, Exercise 2. Page 21.

Answers will vary. These are our suggestions for the first three.
1.   Oh! What a beautiful morning.
2.   Hello, I haven't seen you for so long.
3.   Gee, tell me more.

• Interjections, Exercise 3. Page 21.

Answers will vary. These are our suggestions for the first three.
1.   <u>Ow</u>! I skinned my elbow.
2.   <u>Bravo</u>, what a fine job!
3.   <u>Watch out!</u> That animal is dangerous.

Final Assessment Test, Page 22.

• Prepositions, Exercise A.

1.   He got home <u>about</u> noon.
2.   We returned home too late <u>for</u> lunch.
3.   She stood <u>behind </u>the counter <u>with</u> her hands clasped.
4.   My mother was <u>beside</u> herself <u>with </u>worry.
5.   Take this package <u>to </u>the post office, please.

• Prepositions, Exercise B. .

1.   <u>about the game</u>. >*read*
2.   <u>in the newspaper</u> <u>in the Sports Section</u>. > *was* / > *was*
3.   <u>of Coach Fletcher</u> > *picture* / <u>from the high school</u>. > *Coach Fletcher*
4.   <u>in town</u> > *Everybody* / <u>of the team</u>. > *was proud*
5.   <u>for the team</u> <u>in the Spring</u>. > *trying out* / > *trying out*

• Prepositions, Exercise C.

1.   The puppy with floppy ears ran after the children.
2.   The little girl with a pony tail went swimming in the pond.
3.   A friend from my English class gave a speech to the assembly.
4.   My brother laughed at my sister in the last row.
5.   Dana will be old enough to drive in about five years.

• Coordinating Conjunctions, Exercise A.

1.   My neighbor has two cats <u>and</u> a dog.
2.   I like playing baseball <u>and</u> reading books.
3.   My mother went to the store, <u>but</u> Daddy went to the gas station.
4.   Are you from Canada <u>or</u> the United States?
5.   She said I could go to the movies, the play, <u>or</u> the symphony.

31

• Correlative Conjunctions, Exercise B.

    1.   <u>Either</u> my sister comes with us, <u>or</u> I stay home.
    2.   He was <u>neither</u> short <u>nor</u> tall, <u>neither</u> fat <u>nor</u> thin.
    3.   We weren't sure <u>whether or not</u> he agreed with us..
    4.   Annie <u>and</u> Bart <u>both</u> sat down.
    5.   You can get <u>either</u> A <u>or</u> B on your report card, but no C.

• Subordinating Conjunctions, Exercise C.

    1.   My mother went to the store <u>while</u> Daddy went to the gas station.
    2.   I can drive a car <u>when</u> I'm sixteen.
    3.   <u>Wherever</u> I go, I meet the nicest people.
    4.   You may go to the movies <u>if</u> you finish your homework.
    5.   Donna couldn't go <u>because</u> she didn't finish her homework.

• Interjections, Exercise A.
Answers will vary. Here are some suggestions.

    1.   Hooray! We won the pennant!
    2.   Ooh! I'm so mad that Bob asked Patricia to the Prom.
    3.   Sorry, I broke the window with my baseball.
    4.   Look at the butterfly. Beautiful!
    5.   Mmmm! That cake sure looks good.

Math Series

The Straight Forward Math Series

is systematic, first diagnosing skill levels, then *practice*, periodic *review*, and *testing*.

Blackline

The Advanced Straight Forward Math Series

is a higher level system to diagnose, practice, review, and test skills.

Blackline

Large Editions

Blackline

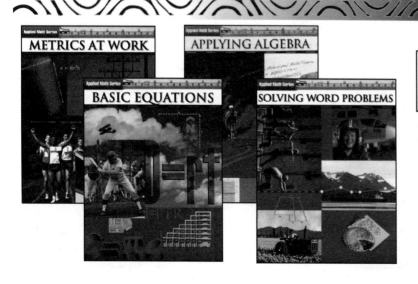

Applied Math Series

The Applied Math Series

is designed for those who wonder how various mathematic disciplines can be used to solve everyday problems.

English Series

The Straight Forward English Series

is designed to measure, teach, review, and master specified English skills: capitalization and punctuation; nouns and pronouns; verbs; adjectives and adverbs; prepositions, conjunctions and interjections; sentences; clauses and phrases, and mechanics.

Each workbook is a simple, straightforward approach to learning English skills. Skills are keyed to major school textbook adoptions.

Pages are reproducible.

GP-032	Capitalization and Punctuation
GP-033	Nouns and Pronouns
GP-034	Verbs
GP-035	Adjectives and Adverbs
GP-041	Sentences
GP-043	Prepositions, conjunctions, & Interjections

Advanced Series

Large editions

GP-055	Clauses & Phrases
GP-056	Mechanics
GP-075	Grammar & Diagramming Sentences

Discovering Literature Series

The Discovering Literature Series

is designed to develop an appreciation for literature and to improve reading skills. Each guide in the series features an award winning novel and explores a wide range of critical reading skills and literature elements.

GP-076	A Teaching Guide to My Side of the Mountain
GP-077	A Teaching Guide to Where the Red Fern Grows
GP-078	A Teaching Guide to Mrs. Frisby & the Rats of NIMH
GP-079	A Teaching Guide to Island of the Blue Dolphins
GP-093	A Teaching Guide to the Outsiders
GP-094	A Teaching Guide to Roll of Thunder

Challenging Level

GP-090	The Hobbit: A Teaching Guide
GP-091	Redwall: A Teaching Guide
GP-092	The Odyssey: A Teaching Guide
GP-097	The Giver: A Teaching Guide
GP-096	Lord of the Flies: A Teaching Guide
GP-074	To Kill A Mockingbird: A Teaching Guide